What is a rainforest?

Rainforests contain some of the most exciting environments on earth – home to giant trees, tiny jewel-coloured hummingbirds, wood-eating termites, upside-down sloths and killer piranha fish. Great apes, such as chimpanzees and orang-utans, also live there.

▶ *A damp mist hangs over the lush rainforest in Chiapas, Mexico.*

Rainforest words

Here are some important rainforest words. See if you can find them and discover what they mean as you read through this book:

sustainable	emergent
plantation	ecosystem
canopy	species
creeper	civilization
prehensile	rattan
bromeliad	timber
manioc	extinct
carnivorous	habitat

Rich in wildlife

Rainforests are amazingly rich in wildlife. They cover less than one-tenth of the land on the earth, but contain over half the world's known species (types) of animals (including birds, insects and fish) and plants. Over 1.5 million different animal and plant species have been found in rainforests so far, and there may be several million more waiting to be discovered.

Tropical or temperate

Most of the world's rainforests are found in the tropics (the area between two imaginary lines around the earth called the Tropic of Cancer and the Tropic of Capricorn). These forests are often called tropical rainforests. They grow in areas where it is very warm and very wet.

Some rainforests grow in areas outside the tropics that are cool and very wet. These forests are called temperate rainforests.

This book focuses on tropical rainforests.

Did you know...

'Rainforests' and 'jungles' are not the same – though people often think they are. 'Jungle' originally meant tangled, bushy plants in lowland India. Today, it usually means the dense, scrubby plants that grow after bigger rainforest trees have been cut down.

In some parts of the rainforests as much as 1000 mm of rain can fall in just one year.

➡ *This map shows the areas of the world covered by tropical and temperate rainforests today.*

Tropic of Cancer

Equator

Tropic of Capricorn

■ Tropical
■ Temperate

Rainforest plants

Rainforests are some of the oldest habitats in the world. They contain communities of plants that have adapted, or changed, to be best suited to their warm, damp environment. Over millions of years, different rainforest plants have developed ways of living together in the same area. Some are tall and make their food from sunlight; others take most of their food from the soil and so can survive low down in the shade. A few even catch insects for extra nutrients. Many rainforest plants rely on one another to survive.

Tall, slender lianas climb up strong forest trees to reach the sun; orchids grow in leaf-mould trapped in cracks in tree-bark.

Canopy:
thick, bushy tops of forest trees (24 m)

Did you know...

Plants and animals live in mini-communities called ecosystems. Animals and plants in an ecosystem rely on each other to stay alive.

In the rainforest, plants absorb nutrients from the soil. The plants are eaten by animals. Some animals are eaten by other animals. Dead animals, fallen leaves and rotten fruit decay in the soil and provide nutrients for plants.

Middle layer:
shade-loving trees below the canopy (15 m)

Shrub layer:
bushes and woody plants (4.5 m)

Ground layer:
small herb-like plants (0.6 m)

Forest floor:
dead leaves and mosses (0 m)

Tallest trees above canopy

'emergents' or 'forest giants' (37m +):
these trees grow higher than the trees in
the main canopy

48 m

42 m

36 m

30 m

24 m

18 m

12 m

6 m

0 m

Did you know...

Plants, called epiphytes, cling
to branches in the middle layer.
They do not have roots, but
get their nutrients from the
rainwater and the air.

Insect-eating plants

Pitcher plants have jug-shaped
leaves that contain a special
liquid. They attract insects by
their smell. Insects land on the
edge of the leaf, and are
trapped by its sticky coating.
They slide down into the liquid.
It dissolves them, and carries
the nourishment they contain
to the rest of the plant.

Rainforest creatures

Many kinds of animals live in the rainforest. Different species are found in different rainforests. Each species has its own place in its local rainforest ecosystem (see page 6), and has adapted to survive in the rainforest environment.

Try This! Smart spiders

Trapdoor spiders live in burrows underground, with a trapdoor-like roof. They hide under the roof until they feel the ground moving as another insect walks by. They rush out to kill their prey, then drag it into their burrow to eat it.

Trapdoor spiders 'listen' to their prey approaching by using their very sensitive feet. Imagine that you are a spider, crouching in a burrow. Design a system to let you know when prey is nearby. Do a drawing to show the materials you would use, and how your early warning system would work.

Monkeys spend their lives high above ground in the rainforest canopy. They have hands with thumbs which help them hold on to branches, and some have long, prehensile tails to grip with.

Hummingbirds have extra-long tongues for drinking nectar out of rainforest flowers. Their wings move up to 30,000 times a minute. They are the only birds that can fly backwards.

Parrots and macaws, which live low down in the canopy, have strong beaks for tearing fruit and cracking seeds and nuts.

Rainforest snakes, which live among leaves and branches of the middle layer, are often coloured green for camouflage. One green species, the vine snake, is so thin (about the width of an adult finger) that it looks just like the stem of a creeping liana.

Sloths hang upside-down from branches. Green algae (simple green plants) grow on their fur. This green colouring hides them among leaves and bushes.

Jaguars have patterned coats which make them hard to see among the shadowy leaves and branches of the rainforest floor.

Poisonous spiders, beetles, butterflies and frogs are brightly coloured. This warns predators to leave them alone.

Some frogs live in the pools of water trapped inside the leaves of a bromeliad (a type of epiphyte). This is a safe home.

Parrots   Frogs   Butterflies   Jaguars

Macaws   Spiders   Snakes

HOW MONKEYS WERE MADE

Rainforests are home to people, as well as different animals and plants. As people lived amongst the wonders of the forests, they created stories to explain their environment.

This story was told by the Maya people who lived in the rainforests of Central America between 1000 BC and AD 1697.

O nce upon a time, there were twin boys called Hunahpu and Xbalanque. They lived with their mother, grandmother and two big brothers in a house in the mountains, surrounded by rainforest trees.

The twins' brothers hated the twins. They shut them out of the house and made them sleep in bushes where the thorns scratched them. They ate all the food that grandmother cooked, so the twins had to hunt and eat birds to survive.

The twins had been born with magic powers. They decided to use their magic to teach their cruel brothers a lesson. One day, they went out hunting as usual, but came home empty-handed. 'Big brothers, please help us,' they cried. 'We've found a tree with so many birds in it, we can't catch them all ourselves.'

But the big brothers were greedy, as well as cruel. The birds would be food for a feast! They hurried into the forest where the twins showed them the tree full of birds. The twins shot some with their blowpipes. 'Big brothers! You are taller than us,' they said. 'Please climb up into the branches and bring the birds down!'

Eagerly, the brothers agreed. But as they climbed, the tree grew bigger until it towered high above even the tallest forest trees. Terrified, the brothers cried, 'We're going to fall!' Far down below on the ground the twins laughed, 'If you're really scared, untie your loincloths and use them to hold on to the tree.'

That is what the big brothers did. The long loincloths looked just like tails. And the brothers looked just like monkeys, as they slipped and swayed among the branches, shouting with rage and fear. In fact, they didn't just look like monkeys, they turned into them! And that is how monkeys were made!

Tiger, tiger

Tigers are the largest of all wild cats – they can grow to 2.8 m long. They live in the rainforests of Asia.

Tigers are carnivores (meat-eaters) and have sharp teeth and claws for catching and killing their prey. They are active at night – they can see in the dark about six times better than people can. Most tigers hunt alone, and they can travel up to 16 km a night to find food. A fully-grown tiger can eat over six tonnes of meat in a year. If they cannot find a large animal to kill for food, they eat smaller creatures, such as frogs, instead.

◆ A Sumatran tiger at rest. Tigers are nocturnal – they usually rest during the day and hunt at night.

The Tyger

Below, is part of a poem written by William Blake about 200 years ago.
Like many poets, he used words to do several things at once. His poem admires the tiger's orange coat, which glows like a fire in the night. It praises the tiger's sleek shape, and the mysterious pattern of its stripes. It marvels at the tiger's deadly strength and power. It also asks who designed and created such a beautiful, terrifying creature.

Tyger, Tyger burning bright
In the forests of the night,
What immortal hand or eye
Could frame thy fearful symmetry?

In what distant deeps or skies
Burnt the fire of thine eyes?

And what shoulder and what art,
Could twist the sinews of thy heart?

And when thy heart began to beat,
What dread hand, and what dread feet?

What the hammer, what the chain?
In what furnace was thy brain?
What the anvil? What dread grasp
Dare its deadly terrors clasp?

Did he smile his work to see?
Did he who made the Lamb make thee?

Tyger! Tyger! burning bright
In the forests of the night,
What immortal hand or eye
Dare frame thy fearful symmetry?

WILLIAM BLAKE

Try This!

Blake's poem praises the tiger's 'symmetry'.

Symmetry describes a pattern with two exactly matching halves, like the stripy pattern on this tiger's coat (below).
The pattern is said to be symmetrical.

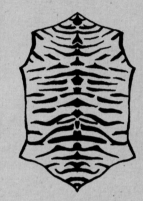

You can use a mirror to create more symmetrical patterns, like this.

YOU CAN TRY THIS!

Tigers in danger

Tigers have been hunted for many hundreds of years. They have been killed for sport, for their beautiful coats and because traditional healers in China and East Asia believed that mixing tiger body parts in medicines would make people strong.

Today, in most parts of the world, it is against the law to kill tigers. But some people still want to buy tiger medicine. They pay poachers – people who illegally hunt animals – a lot of money to kill tigers, even in wildlife reserves where they are protected.

In the early 1900s, there were about 40,000 tigers in the forests of India. Today, there may be fewer than 2,000 tigers worldwide.

▲ *This picture, Tiger in a Thunderstorm, was painted over 100 years ago by the artist Henri Rousseau. He has created dramatic patterns in his picture by showing the tiger's stripes, the heavy, slanting rain, and the huge green shiny leaves of rainforest trees.*

Try This!

Create a rainforest picture using your own patterns of rainfall and leaves. You could use paints or felt-tips, or you could make a collage with leaves cut out of different kinds of paper, and raindrops cut out of clear plastic or silver foil.

Rainforest people

People have been living in rainforests for over 50,000 years. Each rainforest civilization has its own language, customs and beliefs, but they all have many similar ideas about the best way to live.

Survival skills

Rainforest people have discovered ways of sharing the rainforest with animals and plants, and doing as little damage as possible to their environment. They live by hunting wild animals, gathering wild fruit, nuts and insects, and growing vegetables in temporary garden plots. To clear land, they cut down low-growing plants and set fire to them. They leave the big trees standing unharmed. They farm the cleared land for two or three years, then let rainforest plants re-grow again.

▶ *A Caboclo boy from the rainforest in Roraima, Brazil, fishes with a spear.*

▲ *Yanomami people from the Orinoco River basin, Venezuela, farm some cleared land.*

◀ *People from the rainforest in Asmat region, Indonesia, show their respect for the forest through the Sago Tree Ceremony.*

Showing respect

Traditionally, rainforest people looked after their environment and treated it with respect.
In Central America, farmers made offerings to their gods and said prayers before cutting down trees to clear fields for farming:

Lord of the hills and valleys, Lord of the forest, be patient. I am doing what has always been done. I am making an offering, because I am offending against your good will. I hope you will give me permission. I am about to damage you. I am going to work you so that I may live. But I pray that no wild animal of the forest will follow my footsteps, that no snake or scorpion will fall on me from the trees, and that I will not cut myself with my axe as I chop the trees down.

Mayan prayer

Great heritage

Rainforests have been home to many great civilizations in the past.
The Maya are one of the most famous. They lived in Central America from about 1000 BC to AD 1697. They were farmers, fighters, craftworkers and scholars. They built beautiful palaces, and collected treasures of jade and gold.

The Maya worshipped the spirits of their ancestors, and many nature gods. The most important was the sun god Ahaw Kin. They believed that each night, at sunset, he became invisible and turned into a fierce jaguar.

⬆ *The Maya were great mathematicians. This carving shows some of their number symbols. The horizontal line with four dots is the sign for nine.*

Ancient rainforests and rainforest people

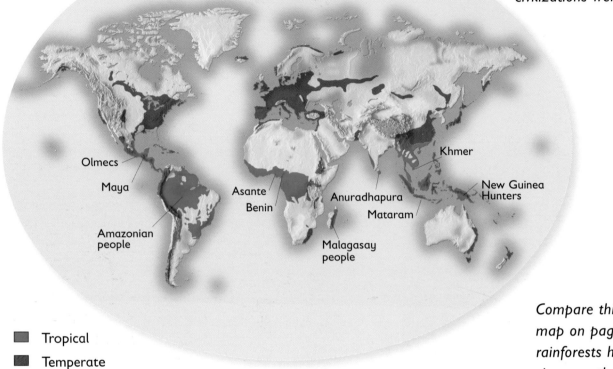

Olmecs
Maya
Amazonian people
Asante
Benin
Malagasay people
Anuradhapura
Mataram
Khmer
New Guinea Hunters

■ Tropical
▦ Temperate

◀ This map shows where some of the great rainforest civilizations were in the past.

Compare this map with the map on page 5. See how the rainforests have changed in size over the years.

Rainforest cities

Today, millions of people still live in rainforest lands. But many of the old rainforest peoples have disappeared, and their lands have been destroyed. Now, many rainforest people lead modern lives. Some live and work in the forests, but many others live in the busy cities that stand where rainforests used to be.

▶ The world's tallest buildings tower above the rainforest city of Kuala Lumpur, Malaysia.

Try This! Mancala

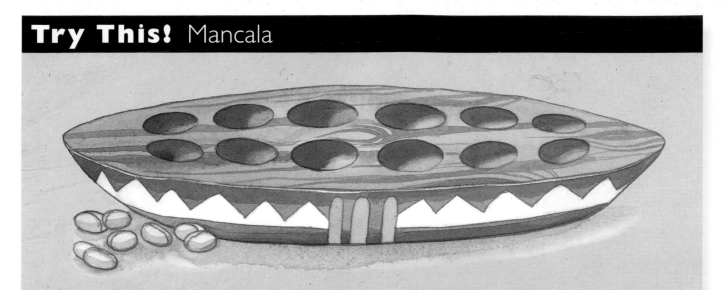

Mancala is a game for two players, popular in Africa. It is played on a wooden board with 12 hollows, using pebbles, seeds, shells or dried beans as counters.

You can make a board out of balsa wood, or clay, or egg-boxes, or just draw one on a big sheet of card. You will need 48 counters. Rules vary from place to place, but here is a very simple version:

1 Sit facing your opponent with the board between you. You each 'own' the side of the board closest to you.

2 Place four counters in each hollow.

3 Start to play by picking up four counters from any cup on your side of the board.

4 Then drop them one at a time into the next four holes, moving anti-clockwise.

5 If the last of your four counters drops into a hole on your opponent's side of the board, you can collect any counters that are already there, and have another turn. Always start from your own side of the board and move in an anti-clockwise direction.

6 If the last of your four counters drops into a hole on your side of the board, then it becomes your opponent's turn to move.

7 The winner is the player who captures the most counters after 10 turns each.

YOU CAN TRY THIS!

Rainforest art, rainforest music

All round the world, rainforest people have created many different kinds of art. Designs vary from place to place because rainforest artists use the natural materials they find all around them. They use rainforest sights and sounds to give them ideas.

Rainforest artists and craftworkers create many beautiful objects. They are designed to be used in everyday life or during special ceremonies. They are often decorated with patterns with special meanings: some designs honour a leader or a god; others show membership of a group.

On these pages you can see two examples of different kinds of rainforest art. Use them to help you to create rainforest designs of your own.

▲ *This mask was made by rainforest people in Africa for use in religious ceremonies.*

Try This! Make a balancing bird

You will need: thin card, scissors, paints or felt-tips, glue or sticky tape, two 1p coins.

1 Copy this picture of a rainforest bird onto thin card and colour it in. Make sure you draw it with its wings outstretched.

2 Cut it out and decorate it.

3 Using glue or sticky tape fix the coins to the underside of the bird's wings – see diagram.

4 Now try to balance your bird on your finger, or on the tip of a pen.

▶ *The Kayapo people of Brazil, use face paint to give information about themselves, such as whether they are hunters, healers or chiefs.*

Rainforest music

Rainforest instruments include flutes and drums – both are made from rainforest woods. This tune is based on a traditional beat from West African rainforests. You could try playing it on the recorder. You could also play it as a round with friends.

To play as a round: player one begins. When he or she reaches 2, player two starts at the beginning. When player one reaches 3, player three starts.

Plants and crops

Many rainforest plants produce valuable resources that can be sold to make money for the people who own the rainforest land. Important rainforest crops include rubber, coffee, cacao (used to make chocolate), palm-oil (used to make soap and other cleaners) and many tropical fruits and nuts. Rainforest creepers are cut, dried and peeled to make a cane-like material called rattan. It can be woven into baskets and chair seats.

⬆ *A plantation of rubber trees in Indonesia. Rubber is made from sap collected from trees.*

Plantations

In the wild, useful plants grow naturally among other rainforest trees and bushes, but it is difficult to harvest them. To make it easier, landowners cut down wild rainforests to make room for huge plantations – areas where dozens of plants of the same species grow side by side, in neat rows. These useful crops are then easy to harvest, but the natural rainforest is destroyed for ever.

Old and new – kola and cola

Kola nuts are the seeds of an African tree. In the past, they were offered to important people as a sign of respect. Today, they are sold by street sellers in many West African towns. Kola nuts are chewed for their bitter juice. They contain natural substances which can stop some people feeling sleepy. When cola drinks were first made, in 19th-century USA, they contained juice from crushed kola nuts. Today, some cola drinks still contain kola nut flavouring.

▶A kola nut growing. Like tea and coffee, kola nuts contain the substance caffeine.

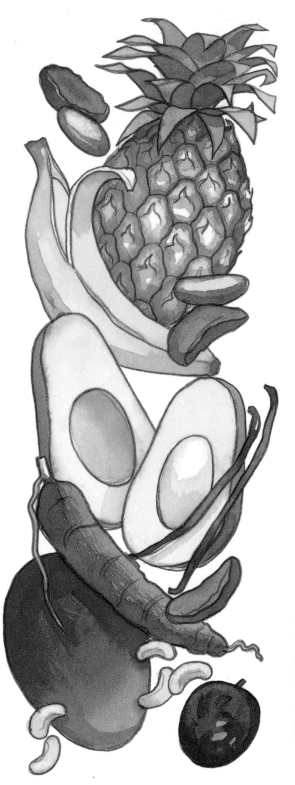

▲ All these foods come from rainforest plants: bananas, pineapples, avocados, brazil nuts, vanilla, manioc, mangoes, cashew nuts and passionfruit.

Try This! Look around you!

Did you know that the tyres on your bicycle, the cane used to make the seats of some chairs, the wood used to make floorboards, tables, chairs and wardrobes, the black keys on old pianos, and many more things might all have come from rainforest plants and trees?

Look around you! How many products can you find in your home or school that are made from rainforest materials?

Rainforests in danger

⬆ *Large areas of the Amazon rainforest are being destroyed in order to build roads.*

▶ *Land is cleared for cattle ranching in the Amazon.*

Today, rainforests around the world are in danger. Rainforest peoples, plants and animals are dying. Splendid rainforest trees are cut down for timber; bushes and creepers are uprooted to clear land for grazing cattle or growing crops.

Forests under threat

Whole areas of rainforest are destroyed by forest fires, or swept away as huge machines drill for oil or precious metals. This destroys rainforest ecosystems – for ever.

Rainforest people are dying from new diseases brought in by people from outside the rainforest, such as ranchers, miners and road builders.

Governments, business people, missionaries and tourists who visit the rainforest do not always understand how these rainforest communities work. Although they are often trying to help, they are destroying the traditional ways of life of the rainforest people.

Did you know...

Rainforest trees help to save land and water. They hold soil together with their roots. They trap water in their leaves and in the dark, steamy space beneath the canopy.

If too many trees are cut down, the soil dries up and blows away and the land becomes a desert.

Global warming

Cutting down rainforest trees damages the environment all round the world by adding to the problem of global warming.

Trees absorb carbon dioxide gas from the air to make food. If millions of rainforest trees are cut down, there are fewer trees to absorb the gas and too much carbon dioxide collects in the air. The carbon dioxide acts like a blanket around the earth, keeping it warm.

Scientists call this global warming. It is changing the world's weather, killing plants and animals and causing dangerous droughts, storms and floods.

◀ *Cleared rainforest land being burnt to provide land for cattle-ranching.*

23

Disappearing species

More than half of the world's original rainforests have been destroyed. Rare rainforest animals are killed by poachers or poisoned by pollution. Some animals starve to death because their habitat has been destroyed.

If this destruction continues, more and more species of birds, animals and plants will become extinct.

⬆ *This red-eyed tree frog lives in the protected rainforest area of La Selva reservation, Costa Rica.*

Almost like us?

Apes live in the rainforests. Of all the animals in the world, they are the ones most like humans. Like humans, they live in families and belong to communities with distinct territories and customs, they communicate by sounds and gestures; they make tools, they are intelligent and curious.

Many species of ape are close to extinction. Their rainforest habitat is being destroyed and many of them are being hunted for meat.

◀ *Mountain gorillas live in African rainforests. Only about 600 mountain gorillas survive in the wild.*

Why are rainforests still being cut down...?

Because the governments of rainforest countries often owe money to other countries (*see box*). These governments can make lots of money by selling permits to allow rainforest trees to be cut down, and by collecting taxes on crops, such as oil-palm, which are planted when rainforests are cleared. Because of this, the governments allow their rainforests to be destroyed.

Because some big international companies, which drill for oil or cut down timber, are very powerful. Rainforest governments and communities cannot always stop these big companies from damaging the local environment.

Did you know...

In the past, banks and governments in rich countries have loaned money to poor countries. The governments of poor countries have used this money to buy things. The money may have been used to build airports or schools, or for buying guns and planes.

Today, many poor countries cannot afford to repay the money that they borrowed. To raise money, they sometimes sell permits to companies which cut down the rainforests. Many people are campaigning for the debt to be cancelled.

Because ordinary people in rainforest countries are often very poor and sometimes have to work for big companies that damage the rainforest so they can afford to buy food for their families.

Because people in rich countries keep on buying rainforest products, such as wooden furniture, without thinking about how they were produced.

Every minute of every day, an area of rainforest as large as 37 football pitches is cut down.

Protecting rainforests

Today, many governments, rainforest communities and international organisations are working together to protect rainforests.

National parks

National parks have been set up where forest people are able to live in their traditional way, and forest animals and plants are protected.

Parks provide jobs for local people who patrol the parks to make sure trees are not cut down, roads are not built, animals are not killed, and the land is not used for mining.

◆ *A teacher shows his students around a rainforest and explains the need to protect the forests.*

A sustainable way

Organisations such as Friends of the Earth and World Wide Fund for Nature encourage the managers of rainforests to use 'sustainable forest management'. This means that rainforest fruits, plants and wood can still be collected and used, but in ways that do not cause long-term damage to the forests.

Local people, such as nut collectors and rubber tappers, are encouraged to work in the forest in a sustainable way, as they always have done. They earn money and pay taxes. This way, the workers and the government both benefit from protecting the forests.

FSC

⬆ *The Forest Stewardship Council encourages responsible forest management.*

YOU CAN TRY THIS!

Try This! What can we do?

We can help protect the rainforests...

🍃 By only buying wood from managed forests. This also helps local people. Look for labels saying FSC (Forest Stewardship Council) on paper, pencils and other wooden goods.

🍃 By buying foods and other products grown and collected by rainforest people working for 'fair trade' organisations. These pay workers a fair wage, which helps to preserve their way of life. Look for 'fair trade' labels on tea, coffee, chocolate and other foods.

🍃 By recycling or re-using wood and paper. This means fewer trees are cut down to make new wooden or paper goods.

What's more...

Jungle children

For hundreds of years, people have told stories about children who have got lost in deep forests, but who have survived because animals have looked after them. Some of these stories may be imaginary, but some are probably true.

In 1920, Reverend J. A. L. Singh, a missionary based in India, reported that he had found children living in a wolf's den deep in the Indian jungle. He brought them back to live in an ordinary home, but sadly they never learnt to speak or behave like other children, and they died young.

▲ *Have you read* The Jungle Book *stories by Rudyard Kipling, or seen the film version? Kipling spent many years in India. He may have written* The Jungle Book *after hearing stories about children found in the jungle there.*

Try This! Write a letter

Find out more about rainforests and the animals that live in them by writing to charities. You could start with these ones:

WWF – UK
Panda House
Weyside Park
Catteshall Lane
Godalming, Surrey
GU7 1XR

WWF – Australia
Level 1
71 York Street
Sydney
NSW, 2000
GPO Box 528

Friends of the Earth
26-28 Underwood Street
London, N1 7JQ

Did you know...

Hammocks were invented by rainforest people who lived in South America and the Caribbean. When European sailors arrived there in the 16th century, they thought that hammocks were such a good idea that they copied them for use on board ship.

When trees were kings

'Going up that river was like going back in the beginnings, when vegetation rioted... and the trees were kings.'

An extract from *Heart of Darkness*, a novel by Joseph Conrad (1857-1924).

These words describe how one man felt as he sailed along a river, into the rainforest.

You could write a poem or a story about how you might feel when you first walked through a dense, beautiful, mysterious rainforest. Or you could draw a picture showing explorers sailing up a rainforest river in a boat. Imagine how they might feel as the tall rainforest trees loomed over them, like giants or kings.

Did you know...

Green plants have a special chemical in their leaves. It is called chlorophyll. It uses sunlight, water and carbon dioxide (a gas breathed out by animals including humans) to make plant food. When plants make food, they give off a gas called oxygen, which humans and animals need to survive. Without green plants, we would not survive.

Try This! Grow a bromeliad

Pineapples belong to a family of rainforest plants called bromeliads. If you have a fresh pineapple, you can try growing the top. But be warned – this is not always successful. Few classrooms or homes provide the rainforest environment that bromeliads like!

1 Slice the top off the pineapple. Plant it in damp compost.

2 Cover it with a clear plastic bag to make a mini rainforest atmosphere.

3 Uncover the pineapple top regularly to spray the pineapple and the compost with water to keep them both damp.

Glossary

adapted: Changed to fit in with, or make the most of, the surroundings.

bromeliad: A family of plants that grow in rainforests. They have tufts of thick, shiny leaves. Some bromeliads are epiphytes (see opposite), others grow on the ground.

canopy: The top layer of rainforest vegetation, formed by the leaves and branches of tall trees.

carnivorous: Meat-eating.

culture: Shared beliefs, traditions and artistic styles of a particular group of people.

civilizations: Peoples or nations who have developed a special culture, language and lifestyle of their own. Civilizations are often powerful for a while, then fade away.

ecosystem: An environment in which all the plants and animals living there depend on one another for survival.

emergent: The very tallest trees in a rainforest, which rise above the canopy layer.

environment: The surroundings – such as air, water and soil – in which animals, plants and insects live.

epiphyte: A type of plant that lives in the canopy of rainforests. It does not have roots, but takes its nutrients from the air.

Equator: An imaginary line that runs round the widest part of the earth.

extinct: Died out.

global warming: A rise in the temperature of the earth.

habitat: The place where an animal, bird or insect lives.

hummingbirds: Tiny, brightly-coloured birds that live in South and Central America and the Caribbean.

jungle: Dense, scrubby plants that grow after bigger rainforest trees have been cut down.

loincloth: Long piece of cloth wound round the body, rather like a pair of shorts.

Glossary

missionary: Someone with strong religious beliefs who spends time teaching other people about them.

nocturnal: Active at night.

nourishment: Food and water.

nutrients: The nourishing parts of animals, insects, plants and soils.

piranha: A meat-eating fish from South America.

prehensile: Bendy and able to grip.

predators: Animals, birds and insects that hunt and kill.

prey: Animals, birds and insects that are hunted and killed.

ranchers: People who raise herds of cattle on large farms called ranches.

rattan: Creepers from a type of palm tree. When dried and peeled, they are used for making baskets and lightweight furniture. Sometimes called 'cane'.

rubber-tappers: People who collect sap from rubber trees. The sap is used to make useful things, such as car tyres.

species: One particular kind of animal or plant, such as an elephant or a banana. Members of a species look like each other, and can breed and produce young. Different species cannot usually breed.

sustainable forests: Forests that are carefully managed. Fruits, nuts and timber are taken from them, but in a planned, thoughtful way, so they can survive.

termites: Insects, rather like ants, that eat wood. Many species of termite live on rainforest floors.

timber: Wood used for building and to make furniture.

tropics: Two imaginary lines drawn round the world north and south of the Equator. They are called the Tropic of Cancer and the Tropic of Capricorn. The area in between them is known as 'the tropics'. Most rainforests grow there.

Index

Rainforest

Fiona Macdonald

FRANKLIN WATTS

This edition 2003

Franklin Watts
96 Leonard Street
London
EC2A 4XD

Franklin Watts Australia
45-51 Huntley Street
Alexandria
NSW 2015

Copyright © Franklin Watts 1999

ISBN 0 7496 4993 3

A CIP catalogue for this book is
available from the British Library

Printed in Hong Kong, China

Series editor: Helen Lanz
Series designer: John Christopher, WHITE DESIGN
Picture research: Sue Mennell
Illustrators: Peter Bull, Sarah John and Carolyn Scrace
Consultant: Dot Jackson

Cover: Bruce Coleman/MPL Fogden (main); Still
Pictures/Michael Sewell (inset)

Interior Pictures:
Illustrations: Peter Bull 5, 16; Sarah John 8l, 10, 12, 17, 18, 20,
28; Carolyn Scrace 6-7, 8-9, 15, 19. Photography: Bruce
Coleman p.14m (Alain Compost), 20 (Alain Compost); FSC
Trademark © 1996 Forest Stewardship Council A.C. p.27t;
Robert Harding p.16 (G. Hellier); National Gallery p.11 *Tiger
in a Tropical Storm (Surprised!)* by Henri Rousseau; Oxford
Scientific Films p.4 (Edward Parker), 14tr (Nick Gordon), 21
(Deni Bown); Still Pictures pp.7 (Dani/Jeske), 11
(Klein/Hubert), 14l (Mark Edwards), 19 (Herbert Giradet), 22l
(Mark Edwards), 22r (Nigel Dickinson), 24t (Yves Lefevre),
24b (Jose Kalpers), 26 (Mark Edwards); Dylan Garcia p.23, 25;
Franklin Watts p.27 both, 29

Quotation p.15 adapted from JES Thompson's, Maya Archaeologist
published by Robert Hale, London, 1962. Reproduced with the
permission of the publisher. For the United States, its dependencies,
the Philippines and Mexico published with permission of University
of Oklahoma Press.
Thanks to the World Conservation Monitoring Centre for map
references for rainforest coverage.

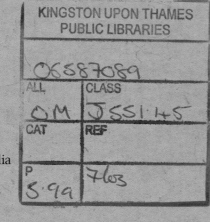
Contents